SCIENCE FAIR PROJECTS

Matter and Energy

Patricia Whitehouse

Heinemann Library
Chicago, Illinois

Customer Service 888-454-2279
Visit our website at www.heinemannlibrary.com

Produced for Heinemann Library by White-Thomson Publishing Ltd.
Page layout by Tim Mayer and Alison Walper
Edited by Harriet Brown
Photo research by Amy Sparks
Illustrations by Cavedweller Studio
Printed and bound in China by Leo Paper Group

12 11 10 09 08
10 9 8 7 6 5 4 3 2 1

Library of Congress Cataloging-in-Publication Data
Whitehouse, Patricia, 1958–
    Matter and energy / Patricia Whitehouse.
      p. cm. — (Science fair projects)
    Includes bibliographical references and index.
    ISBN 978-1-4034-7917-4 (hc)
1. Matter—Experiments—Juvenile literature. 2. Force and energy—Experiments—Juvenile literature. 3. Science—Experiments—Juvenile literature. I. Title.
    QC173.16.W55 2007
    530.4--dc22

                               2006039546

Acknowledgments
The author and publishers are grateful to the following for permission to reproduce copyright material: Martyn Chillmaid, **pp. 6, 14, 29, 34, 42;** Corbis/Reinhard Eisele/zefa, **p. 32;** Ecoscene/Eric Needham, **p. 24;** Istockphoto.com, **title page** (Moritz von Hacht), **pp. 8** (Tan Kian Khoon), **16** (Duncan Walker), **20** (Holly Kuchera), **28** (Gianluca Camporesi), **36** (Jacob Yuri Wackerhausen); Masterfile/Andrew Douglas, **p. 4;** Photolibrary/Gay Garry, **p. 12;** Science Photo Library/Peter Menzel, **p. 40**

Cover photograph reproduced with permission of Josh Westrich/Photolibrary.

 Some words are shown in bold, **like this.** You can find the definitions for these words in the glossary.

Contents

Science Fair Basics

Starting a science fair project can be an exciting challenge. You can test **scientific theory** by developing an appropriate scientific question. Then you can search, using the thoughtful steps of a well-planned experiment, for the answer to that question. It's like a treasure hunt of the mind.

In a way, your mission is to better understand how your world and the things in it work. You may be rewarded with a good grade or an award for your scientific hard work. But no matter what scores your project receives, you'll be a winner. That's because you will know a little bit more about your subject than you did before you started.

In this book, we'll look at nine different science fair projects related to matter and energy. We'll find out some amazing things about how matter is affected by light, heat, and other forms of energy.

Do Your Research

Is there something about matter and energy you've always wondered about? Something you don't quite understand but would like to? Then do a little research about the subject. Go to the library and check out books about the subject that interests you.

Use your favorite Internet search engine to find reliable online sources. Museums, universities, scientific journals, newspapers, and magazines are among the best sources for accurate research. Each experiment in this book lists some suggestions for further research.

The Experiments

Project Information

The beginning of each experiment contains a box like this.

Possible Question:

This question is a suggested starting point for your experiment. You will need to adapt the question to reflect your own interests.

Possible Hypothesis:

Don't worry if your hypothesis doesn't match the one listed here; this is only a suggestion.

Approximate Cost of Materials:

Discuss this with your parents before beginning work.

Materials Needed:

Make sure you can easily get all of the materials listed and gather them before beginning work.

Level of Difficulty:

There are three levels of experiments in this book: Easy, Intermediate, and Advanced. The level of difficulty is based on how long the experiment takes and how complicated it is.

When doing research you need to make sure your sources are reliable. Ask yourself the following questions about sources, especially those you find online.

1) How old is the source? Is it possible that the information is outdated?

2) Who wrote the source? Is there an identifiable author, and is the author qualified to write about the topic?

3) What is the purpose of the source? The website of a potato chip company is probably not the best place to look for information on healthful diets.

4) Is the information well documented? Can you tell where the author got his or her information?

Some websites allow you to "chat" online with experts. Make sure you discuss this with your parent or teacher before participating. Never give out private information, including your address or phone number, online.

Continued

Once you know a bit more about the subject you want to explore, you'll be ready to ask a science project question and form an intelligent **hypothesis.** A hypothesis is an educated guess about what the results of your experiment will be. Finally, you'll be ready to begin your science fair exploration!

What Is an Experiment?

When you say you're going to "experiment," you may just mean that you're going to try something out. When a scientist uses that word, though, he or she means something else. In a proper experiment you have **variables** and a **control.** A variable is something that changes. The independent variable is the thing you purposely change as part of the experiment. The dependent variable is the change that happens in response to the thing you do. The controlled variables, or control group, are the things you do not change so that you have something to compare your outcomes with. Here's an example: You want to test whether salt affects the freezing point of water. You put salt in five cups of water (Group A) and put them in the freezer. You do not put any salt in five cups of water (Group B) and put them in the freezer. Group A is the independent variable. The effect of the salt is the dependent variable. Group B is a control group. Using a large sample of cups for both the variable and control groups will ensure that the results of your experiment are accurate.

Some of the projects in this book are not proper experiments. They are projects designed to help you learn about a subject. You need to check with your teacher about whether these projects are appropriate for your science fair. Before beginning a project, make sure you know the rules about what kinds of projects and materials are allowed.

Your Hypothesis

Once you've decided what question you're going to try to answer, you'll want to make a scientific **prediction** of what you'll discover through your science project. For example, if you wonder why you have to get out of the water at the beach when there's lightning, your question might be, "Does water conduct electricity?"

Remember, your hypothesis states the results you expect from your experiment. So your hypothesis in response to the above question might be, "Salt water conducts electricity." Or it could be, "Fresh water conducts electricity." Your research question also offers a good way to find out whether you can actually complete the steps needed for a successful project. If your question is, "How much electricity is there in the world?," it will be impossible to test your hypothesis, no matter how you express it. So be sure the evidence to support your hypothesis is actually within reach.

Research Journal

It is very important to keep careful notes about your project. From start to finish, make entries in your research journal so you won't have to rely on memory when it comes time to create your display. What time did you start your experiment? How long did you work on it each day? What were the variables, or things that changed, about your experimental setting? How did they change and why? What things did you overlook in planning your project? How did you solve the problems, once you discovered them?

These are the kinds of questions you'll answer in your research journal. No detail is too small when it comes to scientific research. On pages 44–46 of this book, you'll find some tips on writing your report and preparing a winning display. Use these and the tips in each project as guides, but don't be afraid to get creative. Make your display, and your project, your own.

Rainbow Temperature

Stand inside a glass greenhouse and you can feel the heat. The clear glass allows the Sun's rays through to heat up the air, the ground, and the plants inside. The glass keeps the heated air contained. Sunlight is actually made up of a spectrum of colors. Are the different light colors different temperatures? Can you measure the difference in temperature? Try this experiment if you'd like to find out.

Do Your Research

You'll need to do this experiment on a very sunny day. Before you begin this project, do some research on greenhouses and the colors that make up sunlight. Once you've done some research, you can tackle this project. Or, you may come up with your own unique project after you've read and learned more about the topic.

Here are some books and websites you could start with in your research:

» Fullick, Ann. *Seeing Things: Light.* Chicago: Heinemann, 2005.

» Stille, Darlene. *Manipulating Light: Reflection, Refraction and Absorption.* Minneapolis: Compass Point Books, 2005.

» Environmental Protection Agency: The Greenhouse Effect: http://www.epa.gov/globalwarming/kids/greenhouse.html

» Cool Cosmos: Herschel's Experiment: http://coolcosmos.ipac.caltech.edu//cosmic_classroom/classroom_activities/herschel_experiment2.html

Project Information

Possible Question:

Does the color of light affect the temperature of the surrounding air?

Possible Hypothesis:

Different colors of light produce different temperatures.

Level of Difficulty:	Approximate Cost of Materials:
Intermediate	$10

Materials Needed:

» Nontoxic black paint
» Paintbrush
» Five alcohol thermometers, small enough to fit in the cups. You may be able to borrow the thermometers from your school science lab.
» Five large clear plastic cups
» Sheets of cellophane or plastic wrap in red, yellow, blue, and clear, large enough to cover the cups
» Clear tape
» Scissors
» A sunny place to do the experiment

Steps to Success:

1. Use the black paint to cover the bulbs of all five thermometers, and let them dry. Blackened bulbs absorb heat better than clear bulbs do.

2. Cover four of the cups, each with one of the sheets of cellophane or plastic wrap. Use care to completely cover the cup without overlapping the cellophane. Use as little tape as possible.

3. Leave the fifth cup uncovered. This will be your control.

Step 1

POSTER PAINT BLACK

Continued →

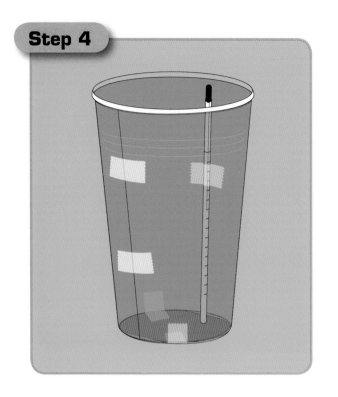

Step 4

4. Attach a thermometer to the inside of each cup with a loop of tape. The bulb of the thermometer should be near the top of the cup, but should not touch it. Be sure you can read the thermometer without moving the cup.

5. Record the temperature in each cup in both °F and °C. (Note: To convert °F to °C, subtract 32 from the figure in °F. Then divide the answer by 1.8. To convert °C to °F, mulitply the figure in °C by 1.8. Then add 32 to the answer.)

6. Place all five cups in a sunny place. Record the temperature in each cup once every minute for fifteen minutes.

Step 6

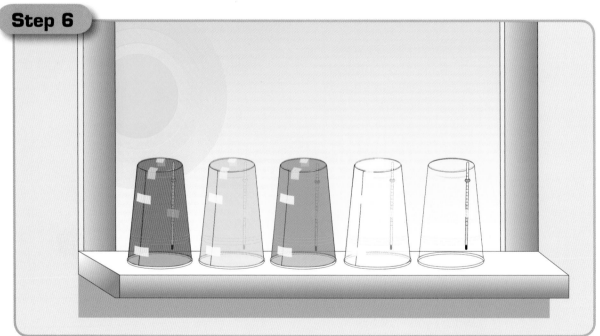

Result Summary:

» Was there an increase in temperature in the cups?

» Did any of the cups show a higher temperature than the others?

» At what time did you notice a change?

» Can you arrange the cups in order from greatest to smallest temperature change?

Added Activities to Give Your Project Extra Punch:

» Repeat the experiment in the same conditions and average your data. Find the average by adding the temperatures for each minute for each color; then divide the total temperature by the number of trials. A greater number of trials will increase the accuracy of your results.

» Try using additional colors of cellophane or plastic wrap.

» Extend the time you collect data.

» Try the experiment on a cooler day and see how the change affects the results.

Display Extras:

» Cover your display board with colored cellophane to form a rainbow pattern.

» Attach the cups you used in the experiment to your board for a 3-D effect.

» Create a border made of suns and thermometers.

» Show your results in both table and graph forms. Choose colors for your graph that match your cup colors.

Warming Up to Magnets

Magnets produce a magnetic field, which attracts some metals, such as iron and steel. Is the magnetic field changed by the temperature of a magnet? Does cooling or heating a magnet affect its strength? This experiment will help you find out.

Do Your Research

This project deals with magnetic properties. Before you begin your project, do some research to find out more about ceramic magnets and magnetism. Once you've done some research, you can tackle this project. Or, you may come up with your own unique project after you've read and learned more about the topic.

Here are some books and websites you could start with in your research:

» Parker, Steve. *Opposites Attract: Magnetism*. Chicago: Heinemann, 2004.
» Vecchione, Glen. *Magnet Science*. Milwaukee: Sterling, 2006.
» NASA: Information About Magnetism: http://www-istp.gsfc.nasa.gov/ Education/Imagnet.html
» Exploratorium: Science Snacks About Magnetism: http://www.exploratorium .edu/snacks/iconmagnetism.html

Project Information

Possible Question:

Does a ceramic magnet's temperature affect its strength?

Possible Hypothesis:

Difference in temperature changes the strength of a ceramic magnet.

Level of Difficulty:

Easy

Approximate Cost of Materials:

$10

Materials Needed:

» An alcohol thermometer or a digital thermometer
» A freezer
» Three ceramic ring magnets
» Six 100-count boxes of medium-sized paper clips
» Plastic tongs
» A heat source, such as a stove burner
» A metal pan and aluminum foil, or an aluminum or nonmetal pan for boiling water, such as one made from borosilicate (Pyrex is a common brand name of this material)
» Water
» Oven mitts
» Adult supervisor

Steps to Success:

1. Put the thermometer in the freezer. After ten minutes, record the temperature in both degrees °F and °C (see page 10 for how to convert between °F and °C).

Step 2

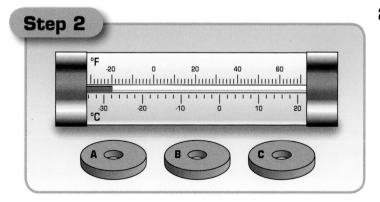

2. Label three ceramic magnets A, B, and C. Put them in the freezer near the thermometer. Leave them in the freezer for ten minutes. Check to see that the temperature remains constant.

Continued ➔

3. Dump out three boxes of paper clips into three separate piles on a flat, nonmetal surface. Separate any that are hooked together.

4. Remove magnet A from the freezer with the plastic tongs and place it in the middle of the first pile of paper clips. Turn it over with the tongs so that it is covered with paper clips.

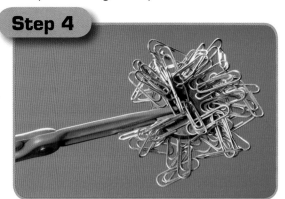

Step 4

5. Remove the paper clips from the magnet. Count and record the number of paper clips the magnet held.

6. Demagnetize the paper clips by dropping them several times from a height of about 20 inches (50 centimeters) onto a table. Return the paper clips to their original pile.

7. Return the magnet to the freezer for ten minutes.

8. Repeat steps 4–7 two more times with magnet A.

9. Repeat the process with magnets B and C and the two remaining paper clip piles.

10. If you are using a metal pan to boil water, cover the bottom of the pan with several layers of aluminum foil. Then half fill the container with water.

11. Heat the water until it is boiling. Boiling water is 212 °F (100 °C).

ADULT SUPERVISION REQUIRED

12. Put on your oven mitts. Use the tongs to place magnet A in the boiling water and let it boil for ten minutes.

13. Set up the remaining three boxes of paper clips as in step 3.

14. After ten minutes, use the tongs to remove the magnet from the boiling water. Repeat the process of attracting, removing, and demagnetizing the paper clips as you did in steps 4–6. Allow the magnet to cool before you remove the paper clips. Return the magnet to the water for ten minutes and repeat this step twice more.

Step 12

15. Repeat steps 11–14 with magnets B and C.

Result Summary:

» What was the average number of paper clips the cold magnet picked up? To calculate the average, add the number of paper clips picked up in each trial; then divide by the number of trials.

» What was the average number of paper clips the heated magnet picked up?

» Did heating change the magnets' strength?

» What can you infer about the magnetic properties of the materials used for making the magnets?

Added Activities to Give Your Project Extra Punch:

» Increase the number of magnets used—more information increases the accuracy of the results.

» Try the experiment using ceramic magnets at room temperature. Compare the results with those obtained when you heated and cooled the magnets.

» Research other types of materials that are used for making magnets, and use them in your experiment.

» Research the Curie temperature and magnetism.

» Research what might happen to a magnet's strength if you could cool it to a lower temperature using dry ice. Dry ice is solid carbon dioxide. It has a temperature of –109.3 °F (–78.5 °C).

Display Extras:

» Decorate your board with a variety of magnets.

» Make an interesting border with chains of paper clips and pictures of thermometers.

» Make a graph to show the results of your experiment.

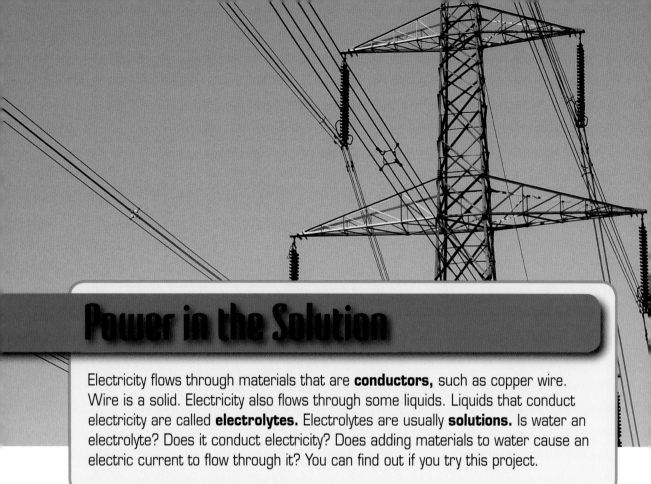

Power in the Solution

Electricity flows through materials that are **conductors,** such as copper wire. Wire is a solid. Electricity also flows through some liquids. Liquids that conduct electricity are called **electrolytes.** Electrolytes are usually **solutions.** Is water an electrolyte? Does it conduct electricity? Does adding materials to water cause an electric current to flow through it? You can find out if you try this project.

Do Your Research

In this experiment, you will need to create an electric **circuit.** Part of the circuit will be the solutions you make. Before you begin this project, do some research on electric circuits and electrolytes. Be sure you do this experiment in a well-ventilated room—small amounts of chlorine gas may be produced when salt water is used as the electrolyte. You'll be making solutions from acids, bases, and salts, so do some research on them, too. Once you've done some research, you can try this project. Or, you may come up with your own unique project after you've read and learned more about the topic.

Here are some books and websites you could start with in your research:

» Oxlade, Chris. *Acids and Bases.* Chicago: Heinemann, 2007.

» Electrolytes: http://dl.clackamas.cc.or.us/ch105-03/electrol.htm

» What is Electricity?: http://www.eia.doe.gov/kids/energyfacts/sources/electricity.html

Project Information

Possible Question:

Does a saltwater solution conduct enough electricity to light a flashlight bulb?

Possible Hypothesis:

A saltwater solution is an electrolyte, so it will conduct electricity. Water with more salt in it will conduct better than water with less salt in it.

Level of Difficulty:	Approximate Cost of Materials:
Advanced	$15

Materials Needed:

» Two **D-cell** batteries and battery holder with clips
» A flashlight bulb in holder with clips
» 8.5-ounce (250-milliliter) glass beaker or cup
» Coated copper wire
» Wire cutters and wire stripper
» Two carbon **electrodes**
» 3.4 ounces (100 milliliters) tap water
» 3.4 ounces (100 milliliters) distilled water
» 2 tablespoons (30 milliliters) salt
» 1 teaspoon (5-milliliter spoon)
» A ruler   » Adult supervisor

Steps to Success:

1. Build an electric circuit by following these steps:

   a. Put the D-cell batteries in the battery holder. Check that the batteries are facing in the correct directions.

   b. Place the flashlight bulb in the holder; set it near the battery holder.

   c. Set the beaker that will hold the solutions between the battery holder and the lightbulb holder.

   d. **Caution: Ask an adult to help you cut and strip the wire.** Measure and cut three lengths of wire; strip the plastic coating from the ends. One wire connects one end of the battery holder to the flashlight bulb holder. A second wire connects the other end of the flashlight bulb holder. The third wire connects to the remaining clip of the battery holder.

ADULT SUPERVISION REQUIRED

Continued

e. One wire coming from the battery and one wire from the lightbulb should be long enough to reach into the glass beaker. Tightly coil each end of these wires around an end of each electrode.

2. Touch the electrodes together. The lightbulb should light up. If it doesn't, check to make sure that each wire in the circuit is connected. Also be sure that opposite ends of the batteries are connected.

3. Fill the beaker with 3.4 ounces (100 milliliters) *tap* water.

4. Place the electrodes in the beaker; be sure they are not touching each other. Note: Each time you put the electrodes in the liquid, keep the distance between them the same. Observe and record whether the bulb is lit. Remove the electrodes.

5. Fill the beaker with 3.4 ounces (100 milliliters) *distilled* water.

6. Repeat step 4.

7. Add 1 teaspoon (5 milliliters) salt to the beaker and stir. Replace the electrodes and observe the bulb.

8. If the bulb does not light, continue to stir in salt in 1-teaspoon (5-milliliter) increments and see if the bulb will light, until you've added a maximum of 5 teaspoons (25 milliliters). Record your observations.

Step 1

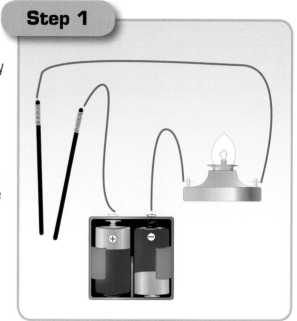

Step 4

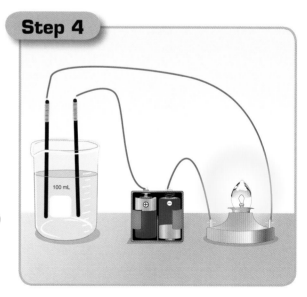

100 mL

Result Summary:

» Did plain tap water or distilled water cause the bulb to light?

» Did the salt water cause the bulb to light?

» How much salt did you need to add to light the bulb?

» Did the light intensity vary as you added salt?

» What factors besides the water's salt content might have affected the results?

Added Activities to Give Your Project Extra Punch:

» Repeat the experiment using fresh batteries and a new flashlight bulb; check your earlier results against this second trial.

» Research the properties of salt and water.

» Add salt to tap water instead of distilled water and report your results.

» Try adding other materials, such as vinegar, baking soda, or cola, to the water.

Display Extras:

» Attach empty containers of salt to your board for a 3-D effect.

» Include photos of your experiment. Label each photo with the amount of salt you used.

» Create a circuit as a border, using wire and a cardboard lightbulb shape.

Hot Cents

Metal is a good heat conductor. If you've ever tried to pick up coins after they've been sitting on the dashboard of a car on a hot, sunny day, you know they can get really hot! But how hot can they get? Does one kind of coin conduct heat better than the others? Try this experiment and find out.

Do Your Research

This experiment deals with heat conduction. Before you begin this project, do some research on conduction, metals, and **alloys.** You'll also need to know which alloys make up the coins you use in this experiment. Once you've done some research, you can tackle this project. Or, you may come up with your own unique project after you've read and learned more about the topic.

Here are some books and websites you could start with in your research:

» Ball, Jacqueline A., and Katie King, eds. *Heat*. Milwaukee: Gareth Stevens, 2003.

» Oxlade, Chris. *How We Use Metals*. Chicago: Raintree, 2005.

» About the United States Mint: http://www.usmint.gov/about_the_mint/index.cfm?flash=yes&action=coin_specifications

Project Information

Possible Question:

Which coin is the best heat conductor?

Possible Hypothesis:

A penny is the best heat conductor.

Level of Difficulty:

Intermediate

Approximate Cost of Materials:

$5

Materials Needed:

» Twelve pennies
» Twelve nickels
» Twelve dimes
» Twelve quarters
» A ruler
» A griddle or flat pan
» Twelve birthday candles
» A stove burner
» A stopwatch
» Two oven mitts
» Metal tongs
» Paper towel   » Adult supervisor

» Cool Cosmos: How Does Heat Travel?: http://coolcosmos.ipac.caltech
.edu/cosmic_classroom/light_lessons/thermal/transfer.html

» Heat Transfer: http://www.bbc.co.uk/schools/gcsebitesize/physics/
energy/energytransferrev6.shtml

Steps to Success:

1. Make stacks of each type of coin so they are all as close to the same height as you can make them. Use no more than four coins in each stack. Use a ruler to measure the stacks.

Step 1

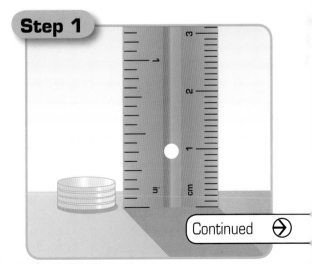

Continued →

21

2. Place each stack of coins the same distance from the center of the griddle. This will ensure that each stack gets an equal amount of heat.

3. Cut a piece ⅓ inch (1 centimeter) long from the bottom of four birthday candles. Place one piece of candle on the top of each stack of coins.

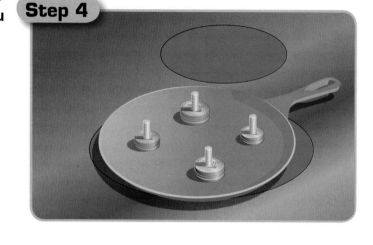

ADULT SUPERVISION REQUIRED

4. Caution: Have an adult help you use the stove burner. Put the griddle on the stove top, turn the burner to the lowest temperature setting, and begin timing the experiment with the stopwatch.

Step 4

5. Observe the candle wax on the top of each stack of coins.

6. Record when the wax begins to melt and when it is completely melted.

7. Turn off the burner when all the wax is completely melted.

8. Caution: The coins and melted wax will be hot. You must use tongs and wear oven mitts for the next part of the experiment. An adult should be present to supervise.

ADULT SUPERVISION REQUIRED

Place a paper towel over the stacks of coins to absorb some of the melted wax. Use the tongs to remove the stacks of coins from the stove top.

9. Repeat the experiment two more times, using new coins and candle pieces each time. Before you repeat the experiment, you'll need to let the griddle and stove burner cool to room temperature. You might need to wait a few hours for them to cool, or you might want to do the experiment on two different days. Record and average your results. To average your results, add together how long it took the wax to melt for each type of coin; then divide that number by the number of trials.

Result Summary:

» What was the average time for the wax to begin melting on top of each coin stack?

» What was the average time for the wax to be completely melted on each coin stack?

» Was there a difference in the time it took for each type of coin? If so, which coin stack was fastest?

» What materials were the coins made from? Be sure to check the date of your coins because that may affect their composition.

» What can you infer about the **conductivity** of each metal alloy?

» What other factors might be involved?

Added Activities to Give Your Project Extra Punch:

» Describe the metals used in the coins you tested.

» Research the type of alloys used for coins that were minted in different years. Include in your report the years of minting for all the coins you used.

» Include additional coins in your experiment, such as a half-dollar coin and a one-dollar gold coin.

» See how your results are affected if you use coins from another country.

Display Extras:

» Show the melt rate in both table and graph forms.

» Decorate your board with enlarged versions of the coins you used. Teacher supply stores that sell units about money are a good source for coins of this type.

» Make a border with play money.

Electric Attraction

Electromagnets use electricity to create a magnetic field. You probably use electromagnets every day because they are inside appliances, telephones, and speakers. They are also used to move large pieces of metal from one place to another. In this experiment, you will learn how to make an electromagnet. Once you do, can you increase its strength?

Do Your Research

Before you begin this project, do some research on electricity and magnetism. You'll also need to know how to build an electric circuit. Once you've done some research, you can tackle this project. Or, you may come up with your own unique project after you've read and learned more about the topic.

Here are some books and websites you could start with in your research:

» Parker, Steve. *Opposites Attract: Magnetism.* Chicago: Heinemann, 2005.

» NASA: How to Build an Electromagnet: http://ksnn.larc.nasa.gov/videos_cap.cfm?unit=electromagnet

» Electromagnets: http://www.ndt-ed.org/EducationResources/HighSchool/Magnetism/electromagnets.htm

Project Information

Possible Question:

Does the thickness of wire affect the strength of an electromagnet?

Possible Hypothesis:

Thicker wires increase an electromagnet's strength.

Level of Difficulty:

Advanced

Approximate Cost of Materials:

$10

Materials Needed:

» 40-inch (100-centimeter) coated wire, thin **gauge**
» A ruler
» Wire cutters and wire stripper
» A large nail or bolt, at least 4 inches (10 centimeters) long
» Two D-cell batteries
» A D-cell battery holder, with clips on either end
» Three boxes of 100-count small metal paper clips
» 40-inch (100-centimeter) coated copper wire, thick gauge
» Adult supervisor

Steps to Success:

Step 1b

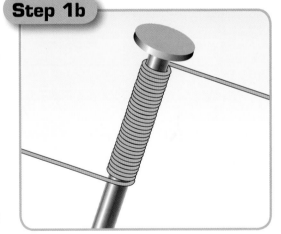

1. Build an electromagnetic circuit by following these steps:

   ADULT SUPERVISION REQUIRED

   a. **Caution: Ask an adult to help you strip the wire.** Strip about 1.2 inches (3 centimeters) of the plastic covering from both ends of the thin-gauge wire.

   b. Tightly wind the thin-gauge wire around the nail, starting about 6 inches (15 centimeters) from the end of the wire. Begin at the head of the nail and neatly coil the wire around to the pointed end. Do not overlap the wire. Make 30 coils in the wire.

Continued →

c. Put a D-cell battery in the battery holder.

d. Attach one end of the wire to the clip at one end of the holder.

2. Dump one box of paper clips onto a nonmetallic surface, such as a wooden tabletop. Spread out the paper clips a bit and make sure none of them are connected.

3. Attach the other end of the stripped wire to the other clip on the battery holder. Your electromagnet should now be working.

4. Touch the head end of the nail to the pile of paper clips. Lift the nail up and move it away from the pile.

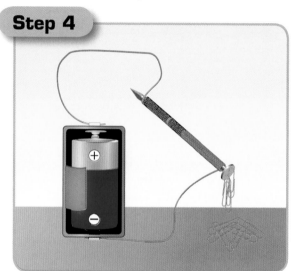

Step 4

5. Disconnect one end of the wire from the battery holder so the electromagnet no longer works. The paper clips should fall from the nail. Count and record the number of paper clips that you lifted. Note: Keep the wire disconnected from the battery holder until you are ready to use it again.

6. Add new paper clips to the pile so there are 100 in the pile. Do not reuse the lifted paper clips because they may have become temporary magnets during the experiment.

7. Reconnect the wire and repeat steps 4–6 two more times. Record your results. Take an average of your results by adding the three results together and then dividing by three.

8. Disconnect the thin-gauge wire from the battery holder and uncoil it from the nail. Put a new D-cell battery in the battery holder. Attach the thick-gauge wire to make an electromagnet circuit as you did in step 1.

9. Repeat the procedure you used for the thin-gauge wire electromagnet (steps 2–7).

Result Summary:

» What was the average number of paper clips each electromagnet picked up?

» Did one electromagnet pick up more paper clips than the other?

» What other factors besides the thickness of the wire might have affected the results?

Added Activities to Give Your Project Extra Punch:

» Research the history of electromagnets and electromagnetism.

» Research what would happen to an electromagnet's strength if you used a glass rod or an aluminum nail as the core of the electromagnet. If you are able to find the necessary equipment, carry out this alternate investigation. Compare these results with the original results.

Display Extras:

» Include photos of your electromagnets as part of your display, showing the number of paper clips each electromagnet picked up.

» Display the electromagnets you made, along with information about how electromagnets work.

» Research how to draw electric schematic diagrams. Include a diagram of your circuit on your display.

» Make a graphic that shows everyday items that use electromagnets.

» Make an interesting border from loops of wire.

» Attach nails and paper clips to your display board in an interesting pattern.

Bright Ideas

If you were asked to go to the store to buy a 60-watt lightbulb, you might be surprised at the variety of 60-watt bulbs you had to choose from. Do you need a frosted bulb, a clear bulb, or perhaps a soft-white one? Does each type of bulb give you the same amount of light? Does each give off the same amount of heat? This experiment will help you find out.

Do Your Research

You will use **incandescent** lightbulbs in this experiment. They give off light when electricity causes a thin wire called a filament to heat up so much, it glows. Before you begin, do some research on incandescent light and on **lumens.** A lumen is a unit of measurement of the brightness of light. Once you've done some research, you can shed some light on this project. Or, you may come up with your own unique project after you've read and learned more about the topic.

Project Information

Possible Question:

Do different types of incandescent lightbulbs with the same **wattage** release different amounts of heat?

Possible Hypothesis:

Different types of incandescent lightbulbs release different amounts of heat.

Level of Difficulty:

Easy

Approximate Cost of Materials:

$10

Materials Needed:

» A flexible desk lamp
» A ruler
» An alcohol thermometer
» Adhesive tape
» 60-watt lightbulbs of various types: frosted, clear, soft white, and silver bowl
» An oven mitt
» Adult supervisor

Here are some books and websites you could start with in your research:

» Collier, James Lincoln. *Electricity and the Light Bulb.* New York: Benchmark, 2005.

» Matthews, John R. *The Light Bulb.* London: Franklin Watts, 2005.

» The History of the Lightbulb: http://invsee.asu.edu/Modules/lightbulb/meathist.htm

» Why Does a Filament Give Off Light? http://invsee.asu.edu/Modules/lightbulb/filament.htm

» Math: Measuring Light: http://www.gelighting.com/na/home_lighting/gela/students/

A lightbulb's wattage is usually printed on the bulb.

240V
60W

Continued

Steps to Success:

Caution: An adult should be present to help you at all times during this experiment. Do not look directly at the lightbulbs when they are on. Wait several minutes after the light has been turned off and the lamp is unplugged before removing the bulb. Use an oven mitt when removing the lightbulb.

ADULT SUPERVISION REQUIRED

1. Set the flexible desk lamp on a heat-resistant surface, such as a tabletop or countertop.

Steps 3 and 4

Step 5

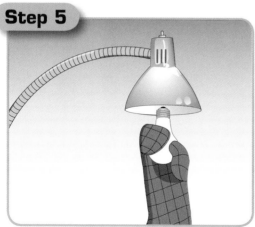

2. Bend the lamp so that the lightbulb is no farther than 6 inches (15 centimeters) from the tabletop.

3. Place a thermometer directly under the part of the lamp that holds the lightbulb. Tape the thermometer in place to keep it from moving during the experiment. Wait five minutes and record the temperature at the surface in both °F and °C (see page 10 for how to convert between °F and °C).

4. Put one of the lightbulbs in the lamp, plug in the lamp and turn it on. Record the temperature every 5 minutes for 30 minutes.

5. After 30 minutes, turn off the lamp and unplug it. Allow the lightbulb to cool before you remove it. Use an oven mitt when removing the bulb. Allow the thermometer on the tabletop to cool to the original temperature.

6. Repeat steps 4–5 using the other lightbulbs.

Result Summary:

» Was there a difference in the end temperature for any of the lightbulbs you tried? If so, what was the difference?

» Can you rank the lightbulbs in order of temperature change?

» Did all the lightbulbs increase in temperature at the same rate over the 30-minute period?

Added Activities to Give Your Project Extra Punch:

» Increase the number of trials for each lightbulb used in this experiment. A greater number of trials will increase the accuracy of your results.

» Look at the lumens ratings on your lightbulb packages. Review your experiment results to determine whether the bulbs with higher lumens ratings produced more heat.

» Use lightbulbs that are labeled energy efficient. Note the effect on your results.

Display Extras:

» Decorate your board with lightbulb shapes that have been covered with bright yellow construction paper.

» Attach the cardboard containers from your lightbulbs to your board.

» Show your results in both table and graph forms.

fun in the Sun

When the temperature is in the 80s, you may think it's great to be outside. But did you know that the air temperature around your feet can be completely different, depending on where you're walking? Some surfaces can become very hot, and the air temperature just above those surfaces increases as well. Above which surface will the air temperature change the most? Bring your thermometers and find out.

Do Your Research

Do this experiment on a warm, sunny day when there is no wind. To get the best results, you'll need to repeat the experiment on at least three days with similar temperatures, so plan your time accordingly. You'll also need quick access to several outdoor surfaces, such as asphalt, concrete, wood, and grass, that remain in sunlight most of the day. Before you begin this project, do some research on the Sun and how the Sun's heat travels to Earth. Once you've done some research, you can tackle this project. Or, you may come up with your own unique project after you've read and learned more about the topic.

Project Information

Possible Question:

Do different surfaces affect the air temperature above them differently?

Possible Hypothesis:

Unpainted metal surfaces will cause the greatest change in air temperature.

Level of Difficulty:

Intermediate

Approximate Cost of Materials:

$5

Materials Needed:

» Access to several outdoor surfaces that are parallel to the ground, such as asphalt, concrete, plastic, wood, metal, soil, grass, and sand. Note: Be careful with metal surfaces in the Sun—they get very hot.
» A bucket or wading pool, and water
» Alcohol thermometers, one for each surface you will test
» Bubble wrap
» Two rubber bands
» A watch or stopwatch

Here are some books and websites you could start with in your research:

» Fleisher, Paul. *Matter and Energy: Principles of Matter and Thermodynamics.* Minneapolis: Lerner Publishing Group, 2002.
» Miller, Ron. *The Sun.* Brookfield, Connecticut: 21st Century, 2002.
» StarChild: The Sun: http://starchild.gsfc.nasa.gov/docs/StarChild/solar_system_level2/sun.html

Steps to Success:

1. Locate the outdoor surfaces you will use for the experiment. They should be close together so you can easily check the temperature at each area during the course of the experiment. A playground or a backyard might be a good location. Be sure that the places you choose will stay sunny during the two-hour time period you'll need for the experiment. You should include at least five different surfaces for your tests.

Continued ➔

2. One surface to test is water. It is safest to use a bucket or a wading pool filled with water. You are testing the air temperature at the surface, so you need to create one thermometer that floats in water. Do this by attaching a strip of thin bubble wrap on the back of one thermometer using two rubber bands. Before doing your experiment test the thermometer to be sure it floats at the surface of the water.

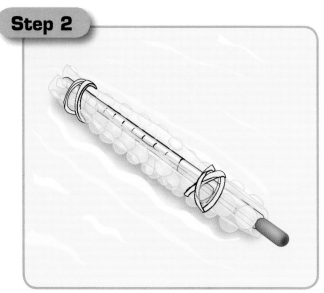

Step 2

3. Set out all the thermometers on a flat surface indoors for five minutes. They should all register the same temperature.

Step 4

4. Place a thermometer on each of your outdoor surfaces. Record the temperature at each location in both °F and °C (see page 10 for how to convert between °F and °C).

5. Observe and record the temperature at each location every ten minutes for two hours.

6. Repeat the procedure on two other days with similar weather conditions.

7. Graph your results for each day and compare them.

Result Summary:

» Above which surface was the air temperature the highest? Above which was the air temperature the lowest?

» If you started your experiment early in the day, did the air above any surface take a longer time to reach the same temperature as the air above another surface?

» What factors, such as the color of the surfaces or the air flow over the surfaces, do you think had an effect on the temperature?

Added Activities to Give Your Project Extra Punch:

» Increase the total amount of time during which you record the temperature changes; increase the duration of the intervals as well. For example, record the temperature every 30 minutes for 8 hours.

» Include additional surfaces in your experiment.

» Research the composition of each material you tested.

» Extend the recording through the evening to determine which location loses heat most quickly.

» Try the experiment at different times of the day and compare the results.

Display Extras:

» Show your data in both table and graph forms.

» Decorate your board with some of the materials you used in your experiment.

» Include photographs of each location you tested.

» Graphically display your results using thermometers copied onto paper. Color the center of each thermometer to the highest temperature you measured in each location.

A Sound Solution

Sound waves are a form of energy that can be a great source of entertainment. Unfortunately, one person's music is another's noise pollution. Earphones or earbuds are a good way to direct sound waves directly to your ears, insulating the sound from everyone else. But what other materials act as sound **insulators?** In this experiment, you will test different bubble wraps to learn whether they are effective sound insulators.

Do Your Research

You'll need a recording with sound on it for this experiment. Your favorite music will work, but it would be better to record about two minutes of a single sound, such as the beep from a smoke detector or the note from an electric keyboard. Before you begin this project, do some research on sound and sound waves. Once you've done some research, you can tackle this project. Or, you may come up with your own unique project after you've read and learned more about the topic.

Here are some books and websites you could start with in your research:

» Isaac, April. *Characteristics and Behavior of Waves: Understanding Sound and Electromagnetic Waves.* New York: Rosen Publishing, 2004.

» Krysac, L.C., PhD, ed. *Sound and Electromagnetic Waves: An Anthology of Current Thought.* New York: Rosen Central, 2005.

Project Information

Possible Question:

Does the size of the air bubbles in bubble wrap affect how well they absorb sound energy?

Possible Hypothesis:

Bubble wrap with smaller air bubbles will absorb sound energy better.

Level of Difficulty:

Intermediate

Approximate Cost of Materials:

$25

Materials Needed:

» A sound source, such as a small battery-operated tape recorder or an mp3 player with speakers
» A cassette tape or similar with a sound of constant volume on it
» Fresh batteries
» Clear tape
» A long indoor space
» A measuring tape
» Sheet of large-bubble bubble wrap
» Sheet of medium-bubble bubble wrap
» Sheet of small-bubble bubble wrap
» Small corrugated-cardboard box
» A **decibel** meter (optional)

» Parker, Steve. *The Science of Sound: Projects and Experiments with Music and Sound Waves*. Chicago: Heinemann, 2005.
» Physical Properties of Sound: http://www.cartage.org.lb/en/themes/sciences/Physics/Acoustics/PropertiesSound/PropertiesSound.htm
» Hearing and Sound: http://library.advanced.org/19537/

Steps to Success:

1. Put your recorded sound and fresh batteries into your sound source recorder. Turn the volume to a low-to-medium setting. Tape the volume control in place so it will not change volume as you cover it with bubble wrap.

2. Place the recorder on the floor of your chosen indoor space. Use tape to mark the placement of the recorder so you can return it to the same place for each trial of the experiment. Turn on the recorder and listen to the volume of the sound.

Continued

3. Move away from the recorder until the sound is very faint or until you can't hear it at all. Measure and record the distance between you and the recorder. This is your control. If you have access to a decibel meter, you can record the decibel level for each trial at the same distance from the recorder.

4. Create three bubble wrap envelopes for the recorder so you can slide it in quickly after you turn it on. Be consistent in the way you cut and tape the wrap to make the envelopes. Tightly seal the joins. Leave one flap of each envelope open until you are ready to use it.

5. Rewind the recording and turn on the recorder. Slip the recorder into the large-bubble bubble wrap and seal the opening. Walk away from the recorder as you did before, until the sound is very faint or until you can't hear it at all. Measure and record the distance.

6. Carefully remove the recorder from the bubble wrap and turn it off.

7. Repeat steps 5 and 6 with the two remaining bubble wrap envelopes.

8. Repeat steps 5–7, but this time cover the recorder with the cardboard box as well as wrapping it in bubble wrap for each trial.

9. Repeat the entire experiment at least two more times. Average your results. To take an average, add the distances for each type of bubble wrap; then divide this number by the number of trials.

Step 5

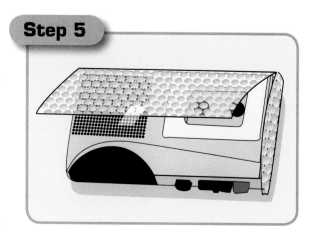

Step 8

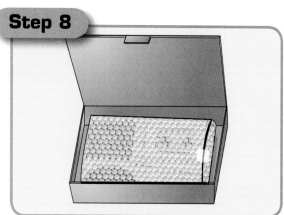

Result Summary:

» Did the bubble wrap cause the sound levels to decrease?

» Did the size of the bubbles affect the distance at which the sound became very faint or inaudible?

» How did covering the recorder with the box affect the sound levels?

Added Activities to Give Your Project Extra Punch:

» Try other materials to soundproof the recorder, such as egg cartons or papers of different thicknesses.

» Research the materials used to soundproof a recording studio.

» Research decibels and how a decibel meter is used.

Display Extras:

» Show your results in both table and chart forms.

» Make a diagram of the place in which you carried out the experiment. For each trial, indicate the spot at which you ended.

» Include photos of the way you covered the sound source recorder.

» Cover the edges of your board with bubble wrap.

Raising Static

Static electricity causes a number of different reactions. It can cause paper to stick to a comb; it might give you a shock when you reach for a doorknob; and it can even mess up your hair when you pull on a sweater. How strong can it get? Do some materials create more static electricity than others? Try this electrifying experiment to find out more about it.

Do Your Research

Static electricity is created by a loss or gain of electrons in certain materials. It is easiest to create in cool, dry environments, so you will get the best results if you do this experiment on a cold, dry day. Before you begin this project, do some research on static electricity. Once you've done some research, you can tackle this project. Or, you may come up with your own unique project after you've read and learned more about the topic.

Here are some books and websites you could start with in your research:

» Parker, Steve, and Laura Buller. *Electricity*. New York: Dorling Kindersley, 2005.

» The Science of Static Electricity: http://www.thebakken.org/electricity/science-of-static.html

Project Information

Possible Question:

Are some materials better than others for making static electricity?

Possible Hypothesis:

Some materials create more static electricity than others.

Level of Difficulty:

Easy

Approximate Cost of Materials:

$8

Materials Needed:

» A small container of polystyrene beads (the kind used in beanbag chairs)
» Six identical plastic combs
» Squares of wool, cotton, and polyester material
» Plastic wrap
» A piece of synthetic fur

» Static Charge: http://ippex.pppl.gov/interactive/electricity/static.html
» Creating Charges with Friction: http://www.regentsprep.org/Regents/physics/phys03/atribo/default.htm

Steps to Success:

1. Divide the polystyrene beads into six piles of the same size.
2. Set the combs on a flat surface. Handle the beads and combs as little as possible to keep from creating static electricity before you begin your experiment.
3. Pick up one comb without touching the tines. Touch the tines to the first pile of beads.
4. Lift the comb up and move it away from the bead pile. Wipe your hand across the comb to remove any beads. Count and record the number of beads picked up by the comb. This part of the experiment is the control.

Continued

5. You'll be rubbing the three squares of material, the plastic wrap, and the piece of fur along the combs during the experiment. Decide on a method that will be consistent in each trial. For example, you might rub the materials back and forth along the comb for ten seconds, or you might rub back and forth twenty times.

6. Pick up the second comb and the square of cotton material, and rub the material along the comb in the way you've decided to use in this experiment.

Step 6

7. Touch the tines of the comb to the second pile of beads, then lift it away from the pile as you did with the control. Count and record the number of beads picked up by the comb.

8. Repeat steps 6 and 7 using the remaining combs, materials, and piles of beads.

9. Repeat the entire experiment on two other cool, dry days and average your results. To take an average, add the number of beads recorded with each type of material; then divide the answer by the number of trials.

Step 7

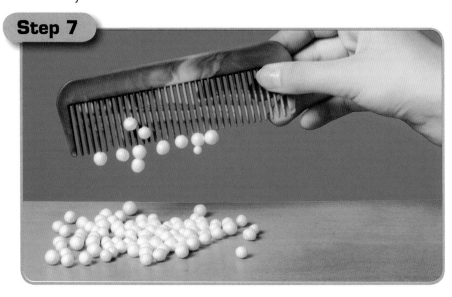

Result Summary:

» Did all the combs pick up beads?

» Were the results similar on each day you did the experiment? Were the weather conditions the same on each day?

» Did one material increase the number of beads the comb picked up? If so, which material was it?

Added Activities to Give Your Project Extra Punch:

» Include research on the **triboelectric** series, a list which ranks how easily materials gain or lose electrons to create static electricity.

» Use additional materials and combs in your experiment.

» Include suggestions for other ways you would extend your experiment if you were to do it again. For example, what would happen if you used combs made of metal instead of plastic?

Display Extras:

» Show your results in both table and chart forms.

» Create a border by gluing a row of polystyrene beads on your board. Glue combs along the top of the beads.

» Include photos of the combs with beads attached to them.

» Attach samples of the materials you used in your experiment.

The Competition

Learning is its own reward, but winning the science fair is pretty fun, too. Here are some things to keep in mind if you want to do well in the competition:

1) Creativity counts. Do not simply copy an experiment from this or any other book. You need to change the experiment so that it is uniquely your own.

2) You will need to be able to explain your project to the judges. Being able to talk intelligently about your work will help reassure the judges that you learned something and that you did the work yourself. You may have to repeat the same information to different judges, so make sure you've practiced it ahead of time. You will also need to be able to answer the judges' questions about your methods and results.

3) You will need to present your materials in an appealing manner. Discuss with your teacher whether or not it is acceptable to have someone help you with artistic flourishes to your display.

Keep these guidelines in mind for your display:

» **Type and print:** Display the project title, the question, the hypothesis, and the collected **data** in clean, neatly crafted paper printouts that you can mount on a sturdy poster display.

» **Visibility:** Be sure to print your title and headings in large type and in energetic colors. If your project is about the Sun, you might use bright reds, oranges, and yellows to bring your letters to life. If your project is about plant life, you might use greens and browns to capture an earthy mood. You want your project to be easily visible in a crowd of other projects.

» **Standing display:** Be sure your display can stand on its own. Office supply stores have thick single-, double-, and triple-section display boards available in several sizes and colors that will work nicely as the canvas for your science fair masterpiece. Mount your core data—your discoveries—on this display, along with photos and other relevant materials (charts, resource articles, interviews, etc.).

» **Attire:** Dress neatly and comfortably for the fair. You may be standing on your feet for a long time.

4) The final report is an important part of your project. Make sure the following things are in your final report:

- » **Title page:** the first page of your report, with your name and the name of your project (similar to page 1 of this book)
- » **Table of contents:** a list of what's included in your report (similar to page 3 of this book)
- » **Research:** the research you did that led you to choose this topic and helped you to formulate your question
- » **Your project question:** what you tested
- » **Your hypothesis:** your prediction of how your experiment would answer the question
- » **Materials:** the things you used to conduct your experiment
- » **Methods:** the steps you took to perform your experiment
- » **Observations:** some of the data you recorded in your research journal
- » **Conclusion:** how closely your hypothesis lined up with the results
- » **Bibliography:** books, articles, and other resources you used in researching and preparing your project. Discuss with your teacher the appropriate way to list your sources.
- » **Acknowledgments:** recognition of those who helped you to prepare and work on your project

Prepare to be Judged

Each science fair is different, but you will probably be assigned points based on your performance in each of the categories below. Make sure to talk to your teacher about how your specific science fair will be judged. Ask yourself the questions in each category to see whether you've done the best possible job.

Your objectives
» Did you present original, creative ideas?
» Did you state the problem or question clearly?
» Did you define the variables and use controls?
» Did you relate your research to the problem or question?

Your skills
» Do you understand your results?
» Did you do your own work? It's OK for an adult to help you for safety reasons, but not to do the work for you. If you cannot explain the experiment, the equipment, and the steps you took, the judges may not believe that you did your own work.

Data collection and interpretation
» Did you keep a research journal?
» Was your experiment planned correctly to collect the data you needed?
» Did you correctly interpret your results?
» Could someone else repeat the experiment by reading your report?
» Are your conclusions based only on the results of your experiment?

Presentation
» Is your display attractive and complete?
» Do you have a complete report?
» Did you use reliable sources and document them correctly?
» Can you answer questions about your work?

Glossary

alloy mixture of two or more metals

circuit path that an electric current follows

conductivity the ability of a material to transfer heat or electricity

conductor material that is able to transfer heat or electricity

control sample in an experiment that is left unchanged and used for comparison with other samples that have variables

data factual information

D-cell type of battery

decibel unit of measurement of the volume of sound

electrode solid conductor used in an electrolyte solution

electrolyte solution through which electric current flows

electromagnet magnet created with electricity

gauge measurement of wire thickness

hypothesis informed guess based on information at hand

incandescent glowing with light when heated

insulator material that does not allow energy to pass through

lumen unit of measurement of the brightness of light

prediction advance statement of what you think will happen, based on scientific study

scientific theory belief based on tested evidence and facts

solution mixture that consists of two or more substances

triboelectric to do with electricity that is produced by friction

variable something that can change; is not set or fixed

wattage measure of the amount of electric power

Index